FLATPICKING SOLOS
12 CONTEST-WINNING ARRANGEMENTS
BY SCOTT FORE

Cherry Lane Music Company
Director of Publications/Project Editor: Mark Phillips

ISBN 1-57560-712-3

Visit our website at www.cherrylane.com

C O N T E N T S

CD TRACK LISTING

Alabama Jubilee
1. Full Performance
2. Play-Along Rhythm Guitar Track
3. Slowed-Down Play-Along

Angeline the Baker
4. Solo Performance

Beaumont Rag
5. Full Performance
6. Play-Along Rhythm Guitar Track
7. Slowed-Down Play-Along

Bill Cheatham
8. Full Performance
9. Play-Along Rhythm Guitar Track
10. Slowed-Down Play-Along

Blackberry Blossom
11. Full Performance
12. Play-Along Rhythm Guitar Track
13. Slowed-Down Play-Along

Cluck Old Hen
14. Full Performance
15. Play-Along Rhythm Guitar Track
16. Slowed-Down Play-Along

Ragtime Annie
17. Full Performance
18. Play-Along Rhythm Guitar Track
19. Slowed-Down Play-Along

Red Haired Boy
20. Full Performance
21. Play-Along Rhythm Guitar Track
22. Slowed-Down Play-Along

St. Anne's Reel
23. Full Performance
24. Play-Along Rhythm Guitar Track
25. Slowed-Down Play-Along

Whiskey Before Breakfast
26. Full Performance
27. Play-Along Rhythm Guitar Track
28. Slowed-Down Play-Along

INTRODUCTION

This book is the result of requests from guitarists who want to learn my contest arrangements. All these tunes and arrangements have been used by me to win various traditional music guitar competitions throughout the United States. Some of the contests I have won with these tunes are the 2003 South Carolina State Flatpicking Championships, the 2002 National Flatpicking Championships (Winfield, Kansas), the 2002 Doc Watson Guitar Championships at Merlefest, the 2002 Galax Old Fiddler's Convention, the 1999 Wayne C. Henderson Guitar Championships (Rugby, Virginia), and many other contests held in Virginia, North Carolina, Tennessee, and South Carolina.

In arranging these tunes I tried to maintain the melody and preserve the flow, but at the same time I tried to use as many "guitar tricks" as possible. To this end, when I arrange a tune, I first learn the melody in as many locations on the neck of the guitar as possible. I also find as many versions of the tunes as I can. And I get ideas from other instruments; in fact, I strive to not listen to guitar versions so that I will not sound like any other guitarist. I also look for what I call the "skeleton" of the tune; in other words, how many of the notes in the melody can I leave out and still recognize it? Once I have found the basic skeleton of the melody and the location of those notes, I begin looking for places where I can insert guitar tricks: slides, hammer-ons, pull-offs, bends, open string/fretted note combinations, chromatic ideas, intervallic phrases, harmonics, etc. There is an endless catalog of musical ideas that are specific to the guitar, and you should be familiar with all of them.

All these arrangements are within the reach of most intermediate and advanced players, but beginning students, too, should be able gain a lot of valuable experience by studying them. The difficult sections can be mastered if you take them one phrase—or even one note—at a time. The tempos indications are a guide, as these arrangements work well at both slow and fast tempos. The main thing to strive for is musicality.

My general rule regarding pick direction is that I use downstrokes on the strong part of the beat and upstrokes on the weak part. With triplets, I sometimes break this rule by starting with an upstroke; in other words, when you have two eighth notes, the first gets the downstroke and the second the upstroke. In a 16th note grouping, the first note gets a downstroke, the second an upstroke, the third a downstroke, and the fourth an upstroke. By following this rule and observing the location of the note within the beat, your pick will always be moving in the correct direction. Syncopations, however, might have you picking consecutive upstrokes or downstrokes.

Good luck, and I hope you enjoy learning these arrangements.

—Scott Fore

ACKNOWLEDGMENTS

I'd like to thank:

My sons, Carson, Austin, and Alex, for love and encouragement, and for being such great sons. I couldn't ask for finer sons and finer people to be around.

My mom and dad for things too numerous to mention.

My brother and sister for years of encouragement and for always telling me that I could do it.

Cheryl Lunsford for love and support. Thanks also for helping me hone these arrangements and for encouraging me to push beyond normal limits.

Carson Cooper for always pushing me to work harder on my right-hand technique and for inadvertently forcing me to keep striving to play with more authority.

Rick Krajnyak at Real2Reel for helping me record the tunes on the CD in his incredible studio, and for friendship.

Lou Roten, Ellen Tait, and Chris Middaugh at Schertler for the greatest pickups and speakers. They help me to always sound good when "plugged in."

Dana Bourgeois, Bonni Lloyd, John Thigpen, and all of the fine folks at Pantheon/Bourgeois guitars for building some of the best guitars found anywhere. Bourgeois guitars bring out the best in my playing and creativity.

Steve McCreary at Collings for supporting the Walnut Valley Festival and for building fine instruments.

Mike Lille and Elixer strings for the great Nanowebs. I exclusively use Elixer Nanowebs strings on all my guitars. Great tone and feel from the time they are put on the guitar. No waiting for the strings to break in.

Wayne Henderson in Rugby, Virginia, for building some fine instruments, and for some fine guitar picking. I feel incredibly fortunate to have the opportunity to learn from great players and builders like Wayne.

All the fine musicians from whom I've had the pleasure to "borrow" guitar techniques. The list is tremendously long.

Wayne Dunford at FotoExpo in Christiansburg, Virginia. Wayne's a great friend, photographer, artist, and musician.

PERFORMANCE NOTES

ALABAMA JUBILEE

This tune, along with "Ragtime Annie," is one that I can always count on to place me in competitions. I use every technique except harmonics in this arrangement. I also normally play this tune at a tempo of 140+ when I compete. This is probably the most challenging arrangement in the book.

It requires you to have a highly developed right-hand technique, especially when playing at the faster tempos, but it also works well at slower tempos.

The song kicks off with the turnaround and goes straight to the melody. The first section is straightforward, and it is not until you get to the second break that things get harder. The second break is crosspicked and there is a lot of string skipping—let the strings ring as long as possible to give a fuller sound. The lick at measure 28 is an intervallic type of lick. I borrowed the idea from jazz saxophonists. The main thing to remember, as for all these arrangements, is to play from chord positions.

The third section begins at measure 38 and is straightforward. Pay attention to the recording to get the feel of the double stops at measures 42, 49, 50, 51, and 52.

Listen to the recording to get the accents.

ANGELINE THE BAKER

The Intro is something I came up with while sitting at a friend's house—I thought it sounded like a fragment of the melody. It is also a way of starting the tune without resorting to the standard "breakdown" type of Intro. The arrangement is fairly straightforward. Try to maintain the flow of the melody since this is a solo. You will note that there is not a rhythm track for this tune.

The first tricky licks come in measures 35 and 39. After the initial bend, rake your pick back across the strings fretted at the 7th fret. This lick is derived from piano players and guitarists like Jerry Reed and Jim Hurst, and I used it a lot when I played electric guitar in country bands in the '80s and '90s. The section beginning with measure 41 is reminiscent of Chuck Berry's licks or those of R&B guitarists of the '60s. Measure 49 makes me think of a loose Steven Stills–type groove. Play this section loosely and don't pay too much attention to the open strings; your focus should be on the fretted notes. Try to keep the dropped D ringing as much as possible to fill out the sound. There is a lot of crosspicking in this arrangement, and it will reveal any weaknesses in your right-hand technique.

The song finishes the way it begins, with the opening chordal structure. You should try to imitate the sound of a slide guitar in the final chord of the song.

As in all the songs, listen to the recording to get the accents. In all these transcriptions, the accents set the notes apart from just a steady string of 16th notes.

Don't let the tab scare you, because this arrangement is really one of the easier ones. The secret to this tune is to keep the open D and A strings ringing in a "drone-like" fashion. This helps fill out the single-note melody line. As with all of the arrangements in this book, play out of the chord positions—this will make the arrangements finger more easily.

BEAUMONT RAG

This is another arrangement that is fairly simple to play. The thing to keep in mind is to keep the flow going.

There is a lot of crosspicking in this arrangement. As with all crosspicking, you need to find the chord shape and hold down all the notes of the chord. In other words, don't read the tab one note at a time, but in groupings of notes. For example, in the G7 chord in measure 18, you hold down the F note at the 3rd fret for the full measure while the other notes move around it. Listen to the recording for the accents in the crosspicked sections. Accents help bring out a melody when crosspicking.

Be careful to let all the notes ring as long as possible for the "floating notes" section beginning at measure 34. "Floating notes" are combinations of open strings and fretted notes; the ringing open strings produce a harp-like sound.

One of the toughest parts of the song is the diminished run in measure 38; you can look for other fingerings to make this run easier, but I've tabbed it the way I play it.

Measures 50 through 53 should be crosspicked. Look at the finger groupings in each measure, and just slide them down the neck; then play measure 54 as a tremolo. It's fairly tough to go from the crosspicking in measure 53 to the tremolo in 54 and maintain timing. As with all the songs, work with a metronome set to a slow tempo, and work up to a fast tempo.

The ending tag in the last three measures can be played without accompaniment.

Again, as with all the songs, listen to the recording to get an idea of the accents.

BILL CHEATHAM

This arrangement is fairly straightforward and shouldn't pose many problems. It opens with a statement of the basic melody. In measure 19 I begin a break using "floating" notes—you should strive to keep the strings ringing as long as possible to achieve the "floating" sound. In measures 31, 63, and 65 the slashes indicate that that section is to be played using tremolo or very fast strumming. Giving the notes their full values will help with the flow of this and all arrangements in this book.

The thing to keep in mind is that, in all the sections, you should maintain chord shapes wherever possible; doing so will help keep notes ringing and help fill out the song.

The trickiest part of the song occurs in measures 51–58, where I play the tune using harmonics. Harmonics are represented by diamond-shaped notes and are played by lightly touching a string directly over top of the fret indicated in the tab. Trying to make these harmonics loud and clear is difficult at the faster tempos at which this piece is normally played. The song is fairly straightforward after this point.

Again, listen to the recording to get an idea of the accents.

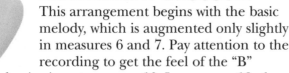

BLACKBERRY BLOSSOM

This arrangement begins with the basic melody, which is augmented only slightly in measures 6 and 7. Pay attention to the recording to get the feel of the "B" section beginning at measure 10. In measure 18, the open G string allows you to move up the neck without breaking the flow of the tune. This is a trick used by lots of guitarists. The open string rings while the hand is changing positions.

The "floating" section, which begins at measure 34, is played by holding the chord shape and sliding it down the neck while allowing the open strings to ring.

Measures 44 and 45 should be played as one long run to maintain the flow. Let the notes ring into each other to achieve that "floating" sound.

The ending, which begins with the last measure of the "B" section, is played as one long grouping.

This is one of the most often-played tunes in the fiddle tune repertoire, and the first tune I learned many years ago.

CLUCK OLD HEN

"Cluck Old Hen" is an old-time modal tune with both a major and minor feel. It's good for learning to use the pentatonic scale to improvise. It's similar to such tunes as "Big Mon," "Wheel Hoss," and others that use a flat-7th chord.

The bends can be played, alternatively, using slides or "hammer-ons." As in all the tunes in this book, let the notes ring for their full values. Listen to the recording to get an idea of the exact rhythms.

Guitarists familiar with pentatonic and blues scales will find this arrangement very "finger friendly." Improvising over this progression is easy when using the G blues scale in its various positions.

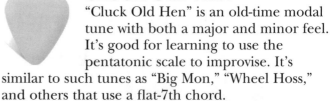

RAGTIME ANNIE

Pay attention to the rhythmic groupings and listen to the recording to get the rhythmic nuances. This is a dance tune and, as such, should be played with dancers in mind. It needs a strong right-hand technique because of the crosspicking involved. As with all the tunes in this book, you should let the notes ring for their full values, if not longer, to give the song a full sound.

This arrangement is a crosspicking tour de force and requires right-hand precision. The piece can be crosspicked using strict alternate picking or the "DDU" pattern used by crosspicking legends George Shuffler and James Allen Shelton. This pattern creates a slightly different sound but also makes it more difficult to achieve the same speed that can be obtained with alternate picking. Depending on the sound I want to achieve, I use both picking patterns.

RED HAIRED BOY

This version is rather basic and should be accessible to all beginning and intermediate guitarists—there are no difficult techniques used. The last section is played mostly with hammer-ons and pull-offs and serves as a good exercise for those techniques. The second break is played mainly around the 7th fret. For the Chorus in the second section, try to think like a mandolinist to get the feel of the chordal section and play it loosely. Listen to the recording to get the accents.

The section beginning at measure 65 may be challenging for some guitarists, as it contains numerous hammer-ons and pull-offs. The challenge is to maintain the volume of the slurred notes. With pull-offs this can be achieved only through proper technique; that is, pull and lift rather than simply lift.

ST. ANNE'S REEL

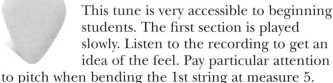

This tune is very accessible to beginning students. The first section is played slowly. Listen to the recording to get an idea of the feel. Pay particular attention to pitch when bending the 1st string at measure 5.

At measure 10, the song begins at the indicated tempo, and the rhythm track begins here. This arrangement is fairly basic until you get to the second section beginning at measure 43. The triplets are played using the hammer-on, pull-off technique. The triplet in measure 58 is played using pull-offs. The "B" section is played using the "floating" chord shapes approach. These chords move around a lot; practice slowly to get the notes to ring out clearly.

For all crosspicked tunes, pay attention to the accents to bring out the melody.

This tune is played out of chord shapes, some of which may be unfamiliar. The key to making this arrangement sound smooth is to find those shapes and hold them down.

Listen to the recording to get an idea of where the accents fall.

WHISKEY BEFORE BREAKFAST

Your guitar should be in drop-D tuning for this arrangement.

Normally this song begins with a pickup (one or more notes immediately before a bar line that begin a melody or phrase). But I have not used one here.

The first two bars of the song and most of the melody are scalar in structure. The first break is played mainly from first position open chord scale forms. I've stayed with the melody, and any deviations are diatonic in nature (all the notes are contained within the key). The slide in measure 21 does not originate from any particular note, although I normally slide from the D at the 3rd fret.

I've inserted two endings for the first break to demonstrate two possible ways to end one break and lead into another. The first takes you back to the first note of measure 1, while the second leads into the second break—you can use either ending, depending on the arrangement you want to use. The 32nd note figure at the end of ending 1 would be considered a pickup figure. Most fiddle tunes end on the first note of the final measure or the third note of the final measure of the break, which leaves one or two beats for the pickup. If you are in a jam situation and want to use one of these breaks, you can use a pickup or just begin on beat 1 of the break.

The second break begins at measure 35. Its first section, which runs to measure 50, is played in 7th position. The second section of this break, which starts at measure 52, begins in 10th position.

Measures 54 and 55 are played using harmonics. Measure 56 begins a sequence of descending 6th intervals—they move diatonically down the fretboard. The section then repeats.

The third break begins at measure 68 and is based on the open string sound called "floating." I've indicated that you should let the strings ring into one another. This section is easier if you notice the note groupings and play as if you are holding chords or chord fragments. The "B" section of this break should be played in a similar fashion. Let all the notes ring for their full values.

Note that measures 100–104 are a Tag to provide an ending for the song.

I've stayed close to the melody in this arrangement and used predominately notes contained within the D major scale. I've done this to show the enormous possibilities that are contained within a scale. You can use rhythmic variety to add interest, as well as such guitar tricks as harmonics, "floating" notes, and slurs (hammer-ons, pull-offs, and slides), but there are many other possibilities as well. You can use pedal tones and play the melody against these. You can even play the melody using harmonic intervals such as 3rds, 4ths, 5ths, octaves, etc. An interesting and challenging exercise is to take every other note and raise or lower it an octave.

ALABAMA JUBILEE

Words by Jack Yellen
Music by George Cobb

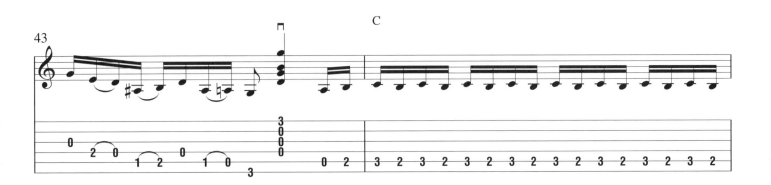

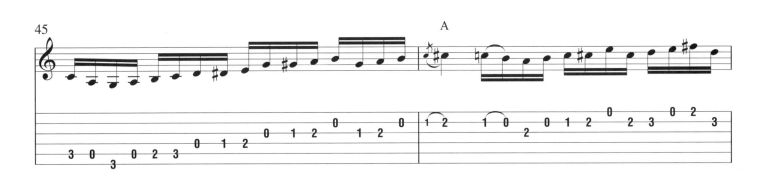

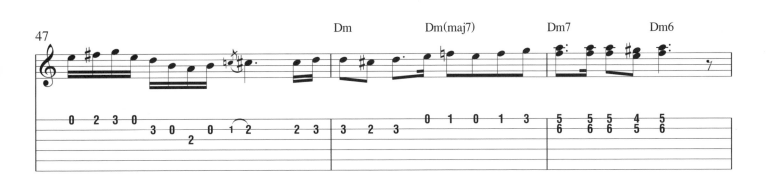

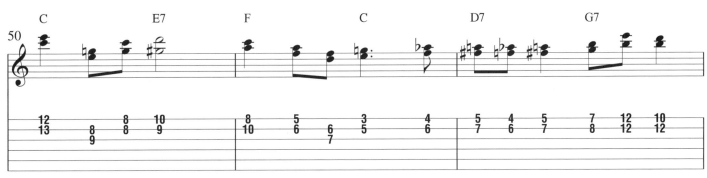

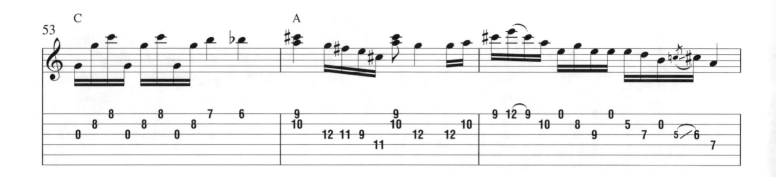

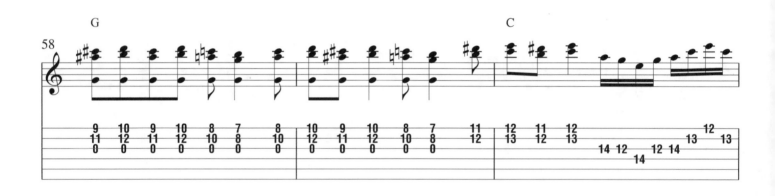

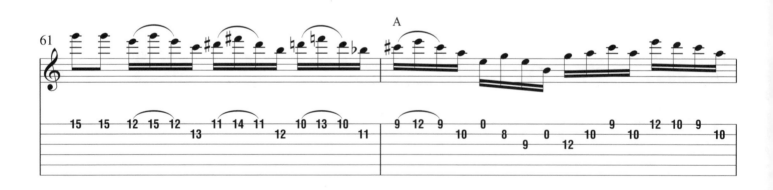

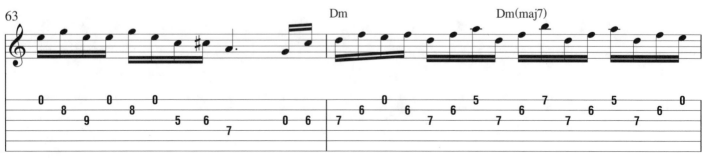

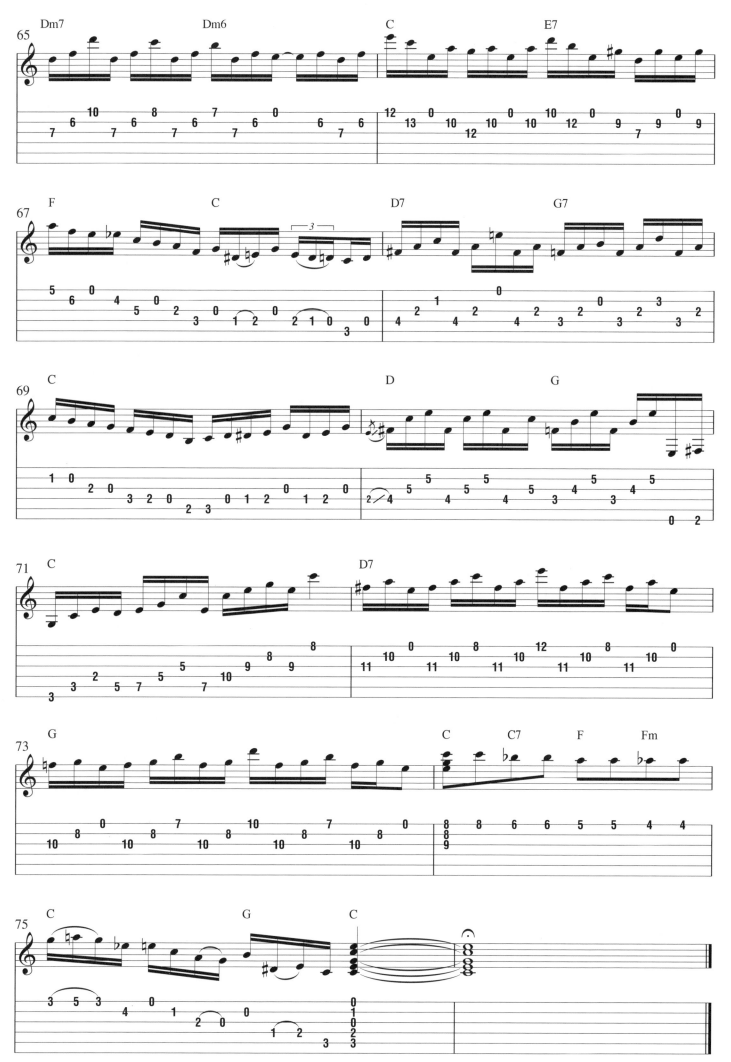

ANGELINE THE BAKER

Traditional

Drop D tuning:
(low to high) D-A-D-G-B-E

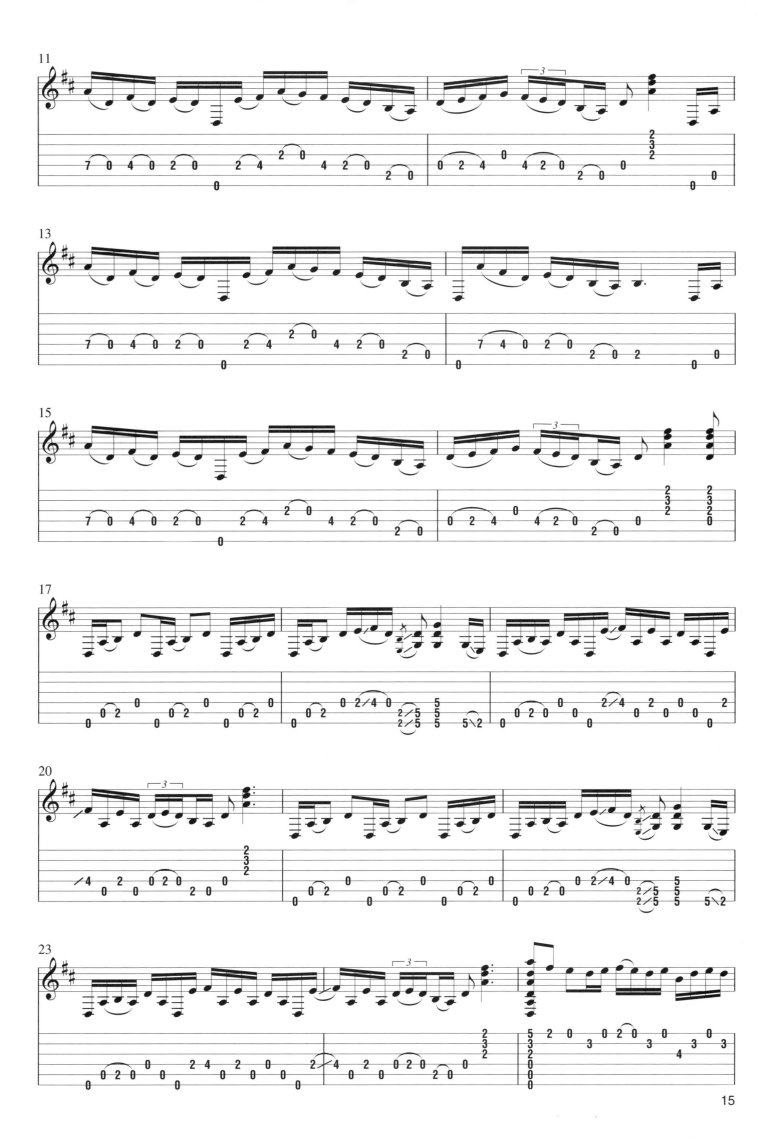

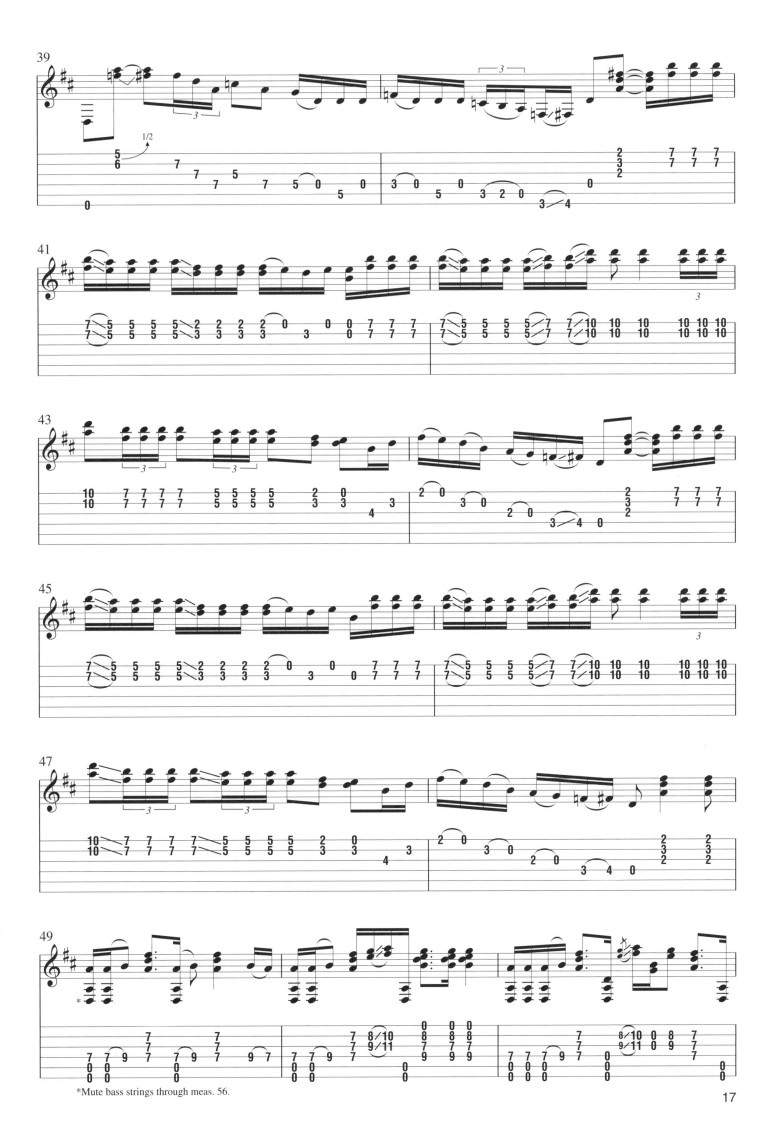

*Mute bass strings through meas. 56.

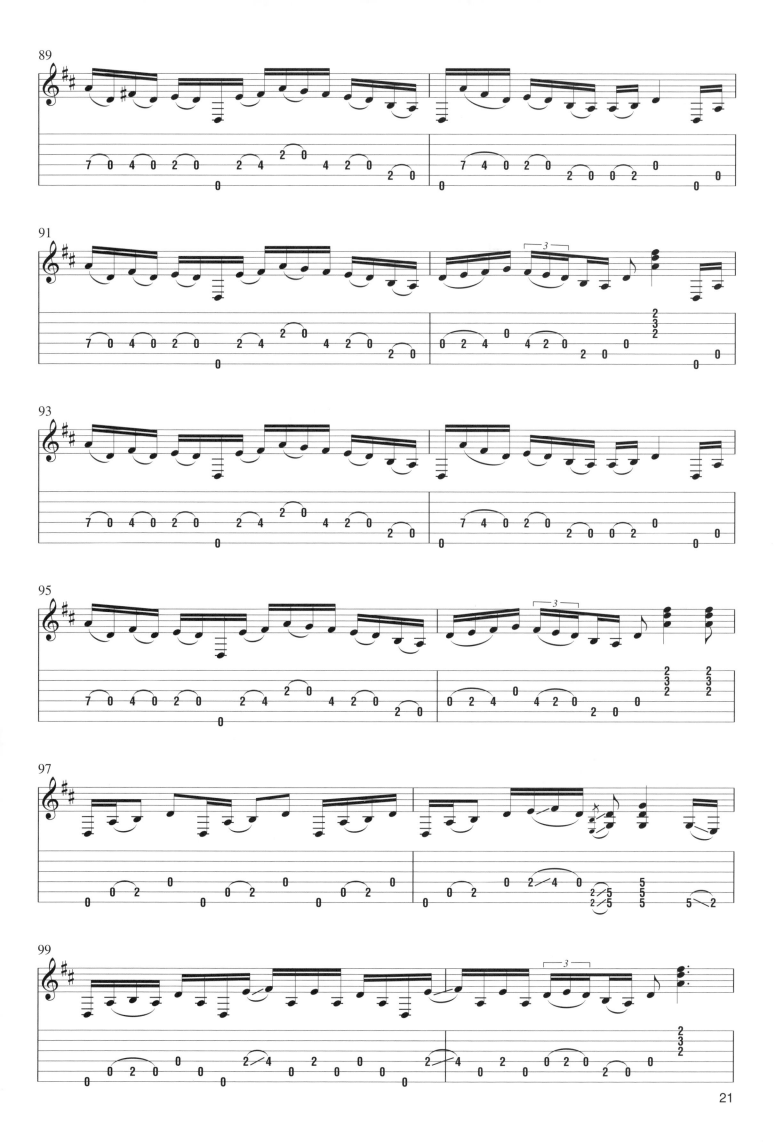

BEAUMONT RAG

Traditional

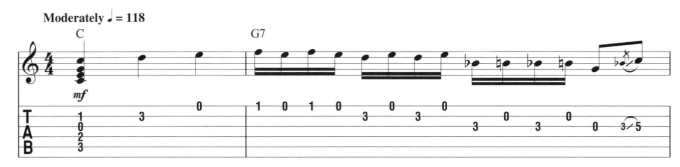

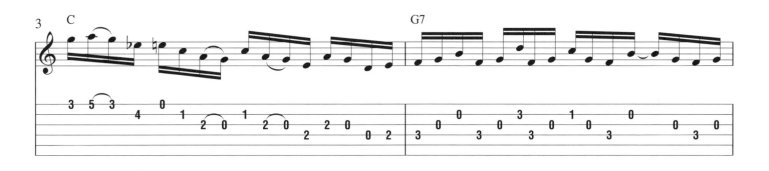

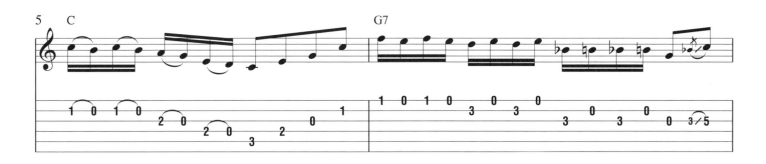

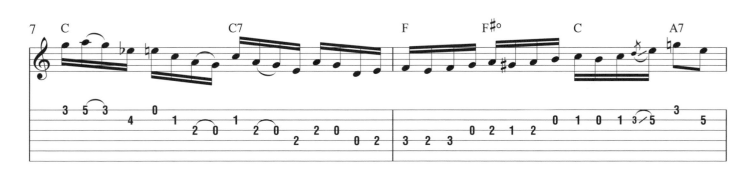

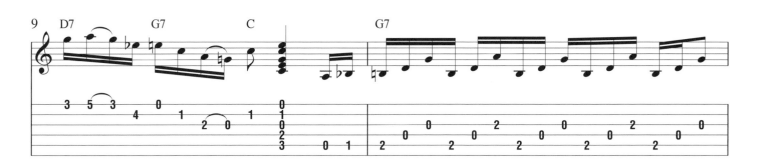

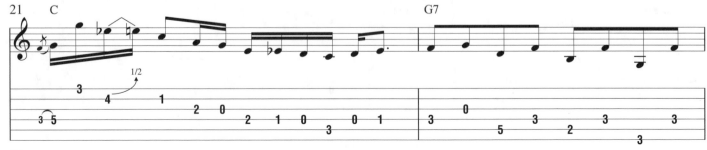

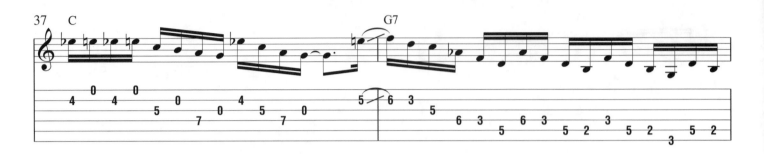

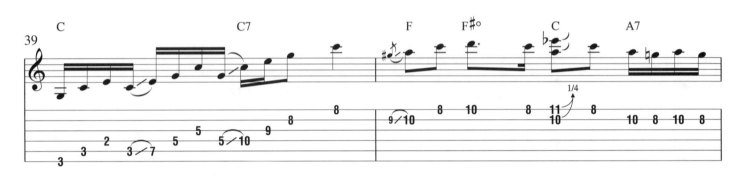

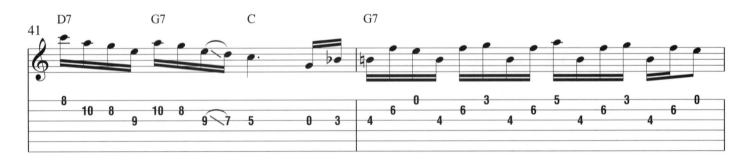

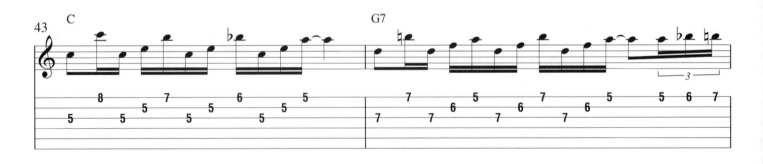

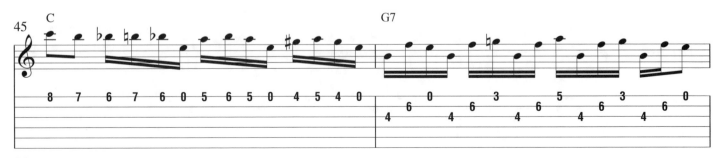

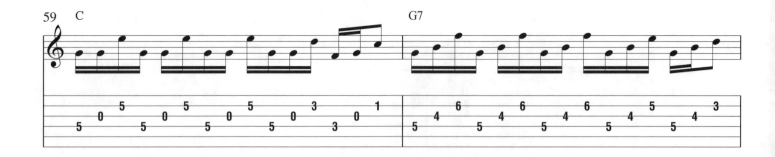

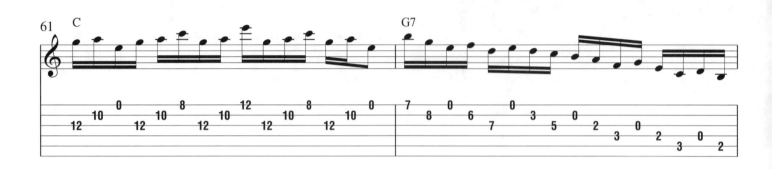

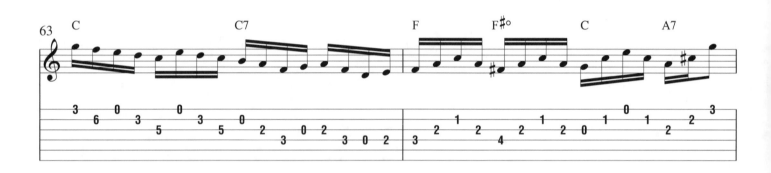

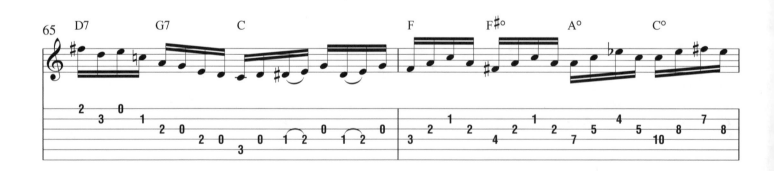

BILL CHEATHAM

Capo II

Traditional

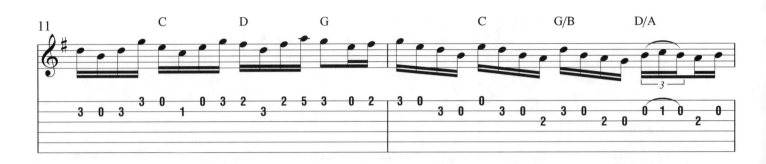

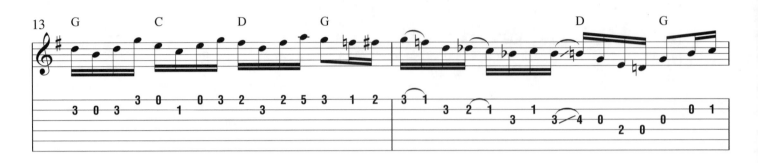

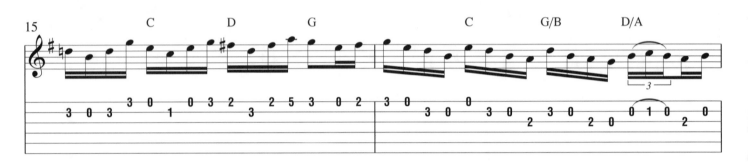

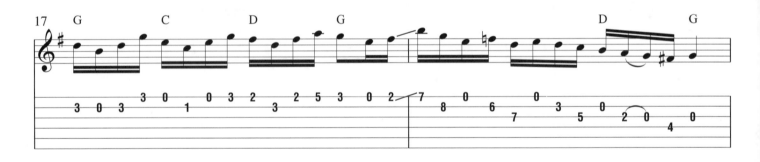

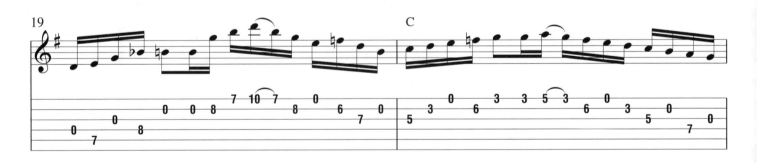

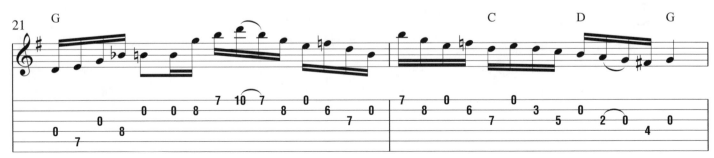

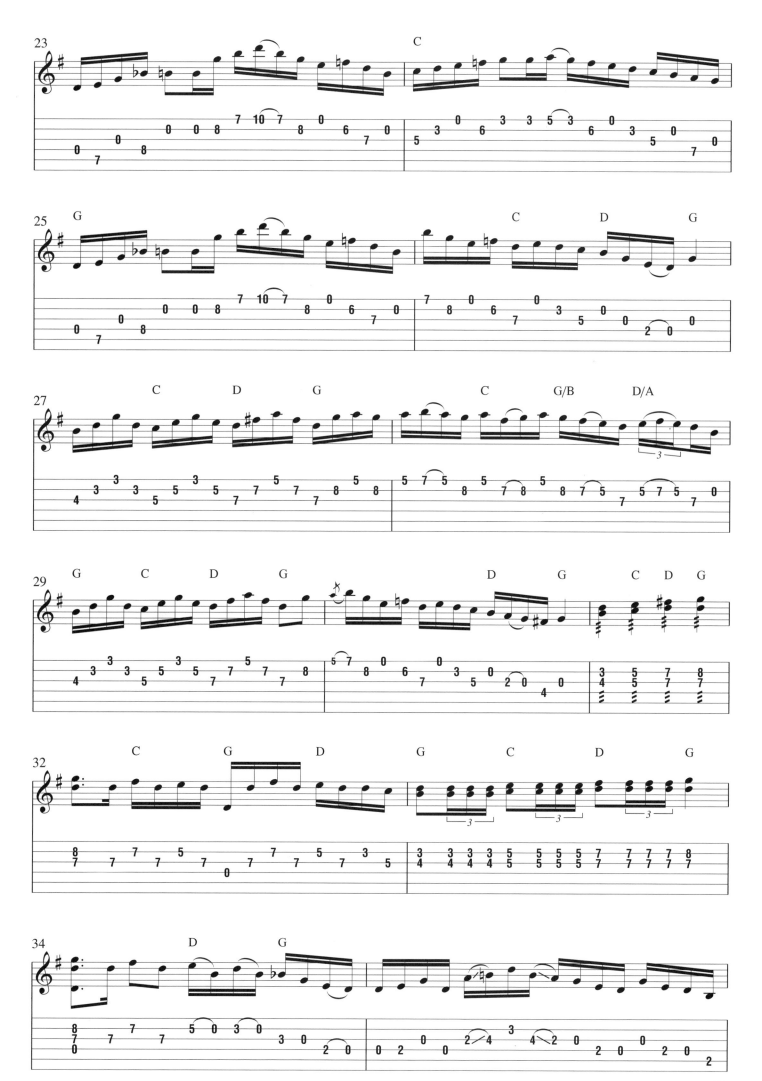

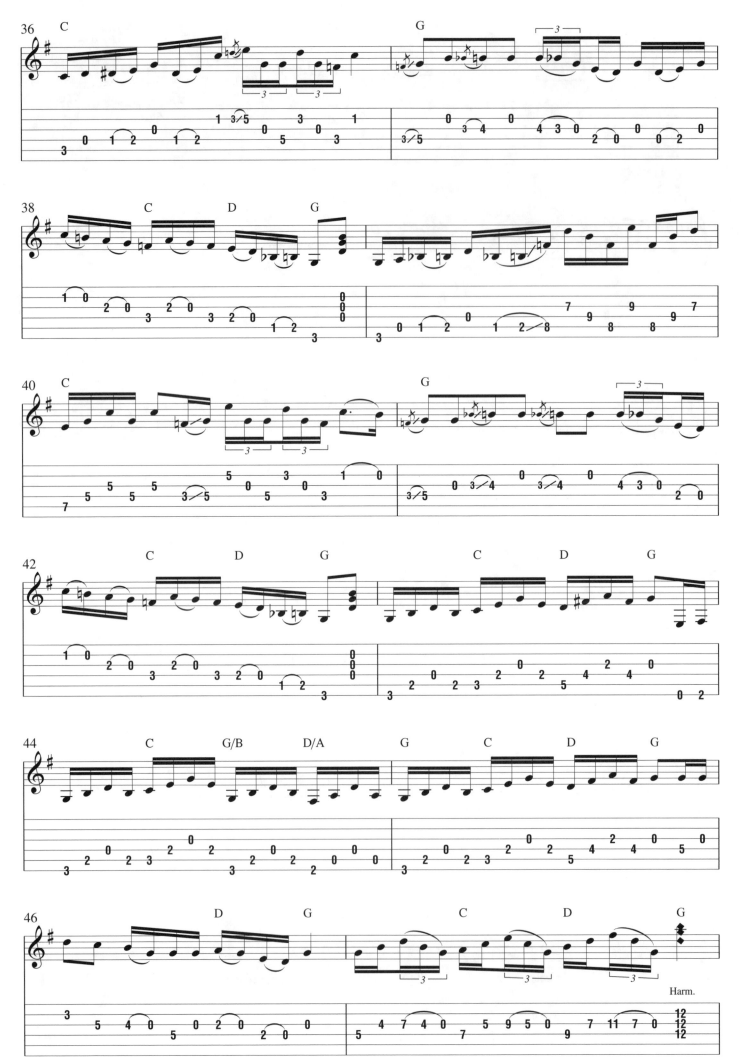

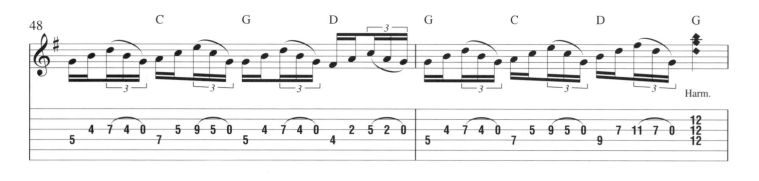

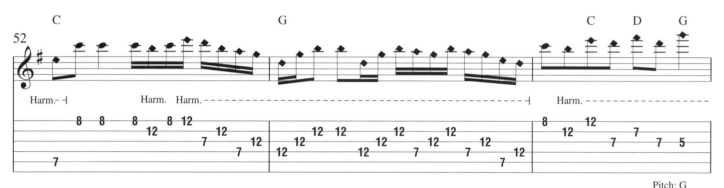

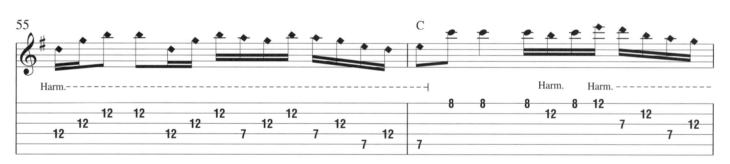

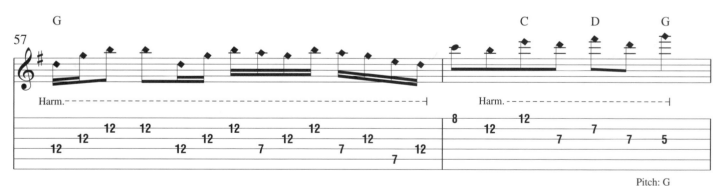

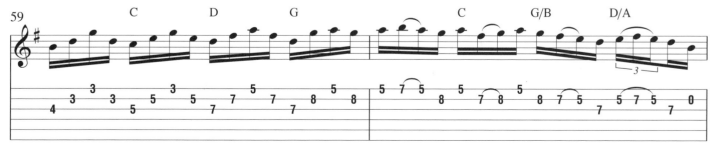

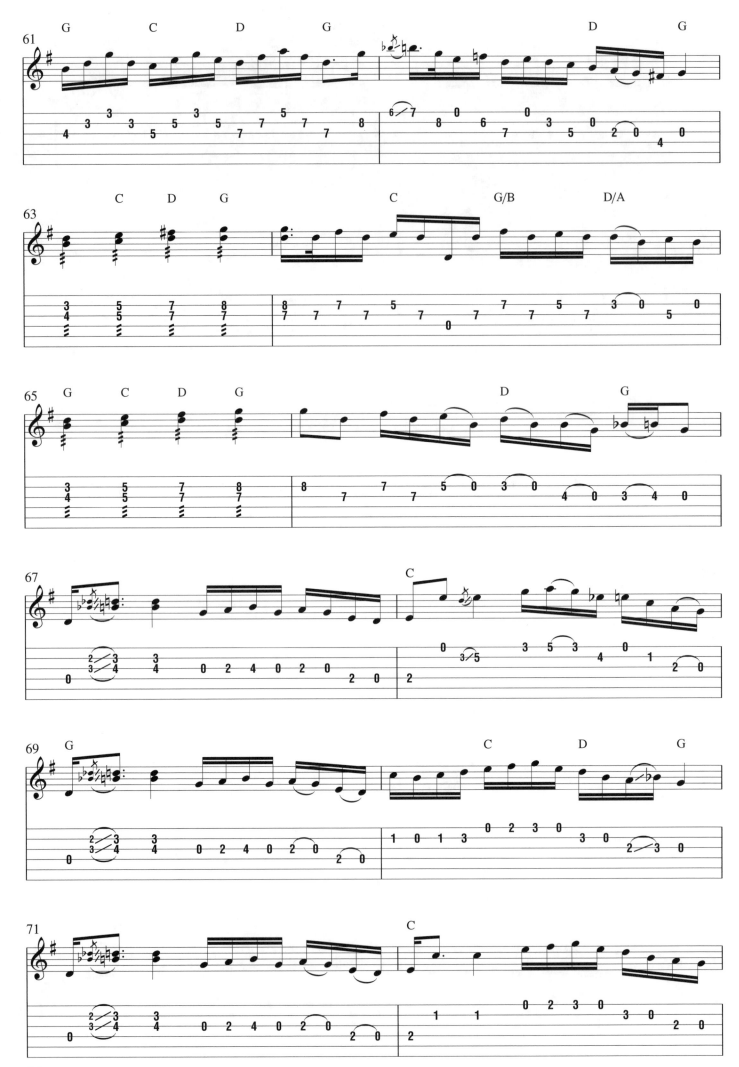

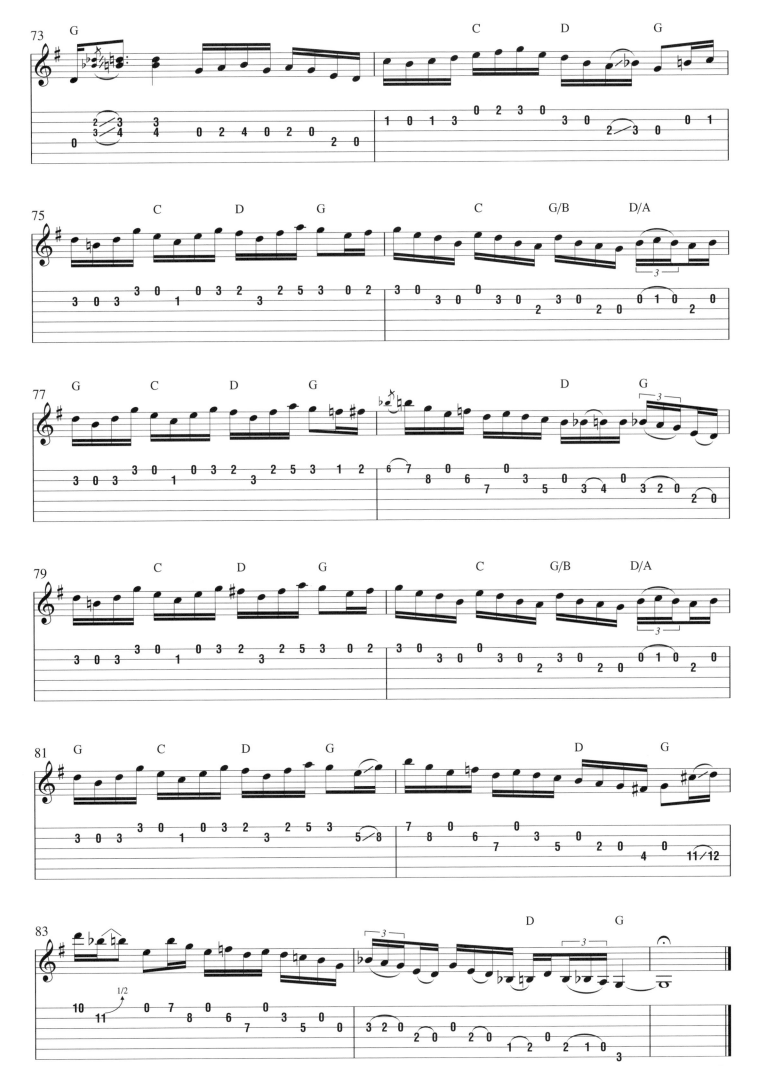

BLACKBERRY BLOSSOM

Traditional

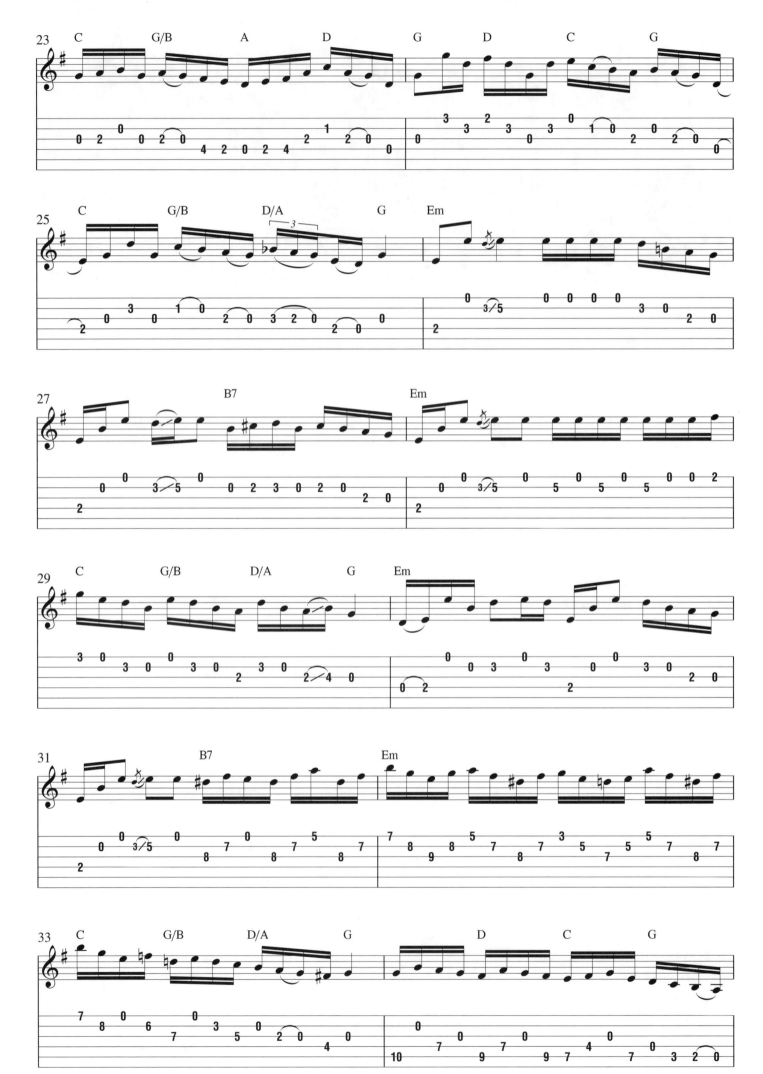

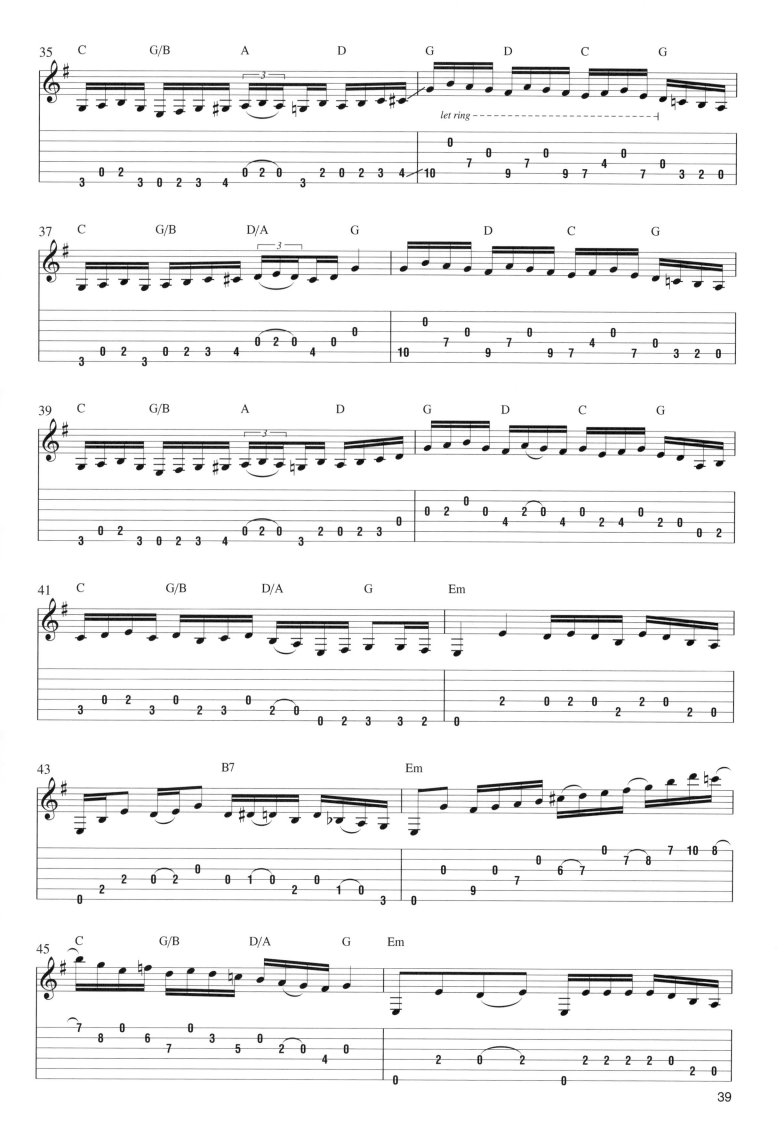

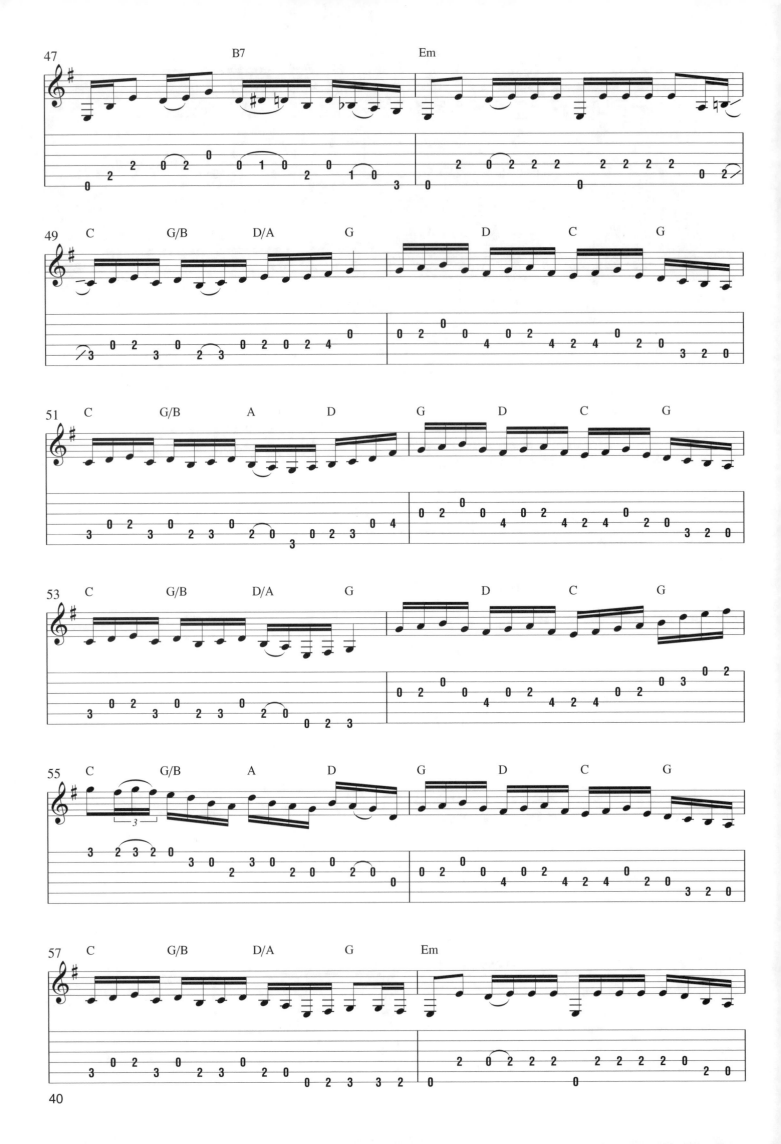

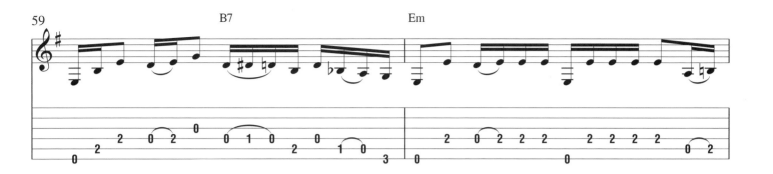

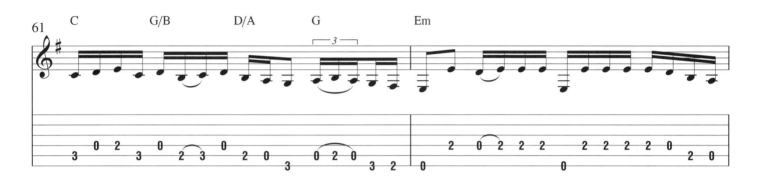

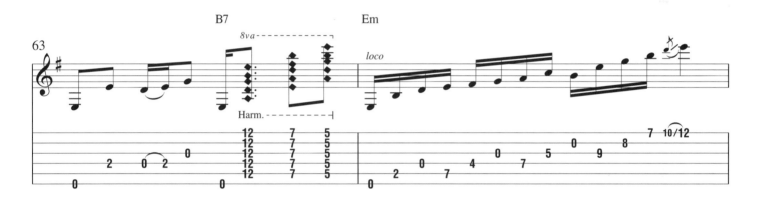

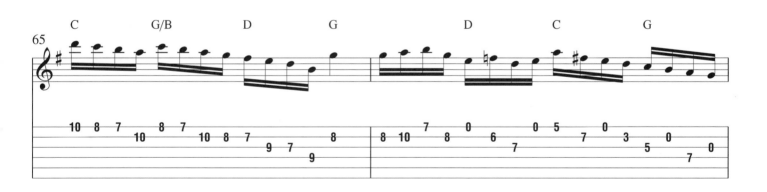

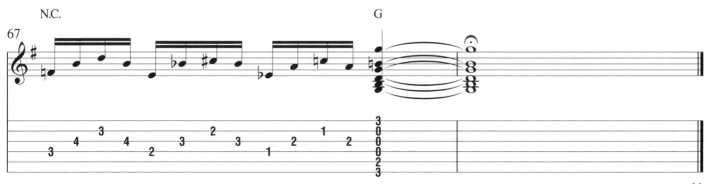

CLUCK OLD HEN

Traditional

RAGTIME ANNIE

Traditional

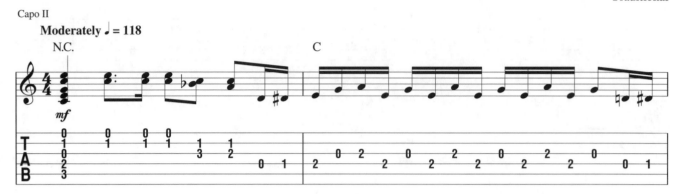

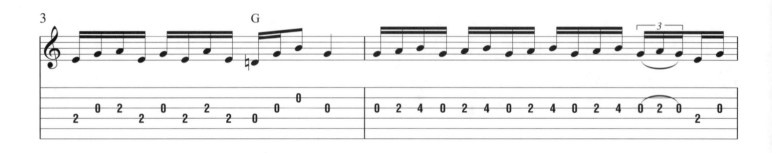

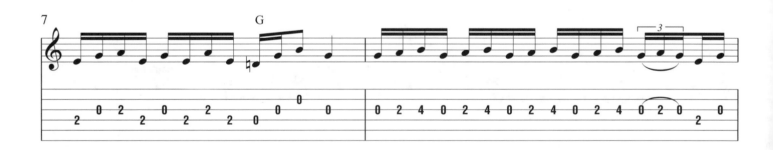

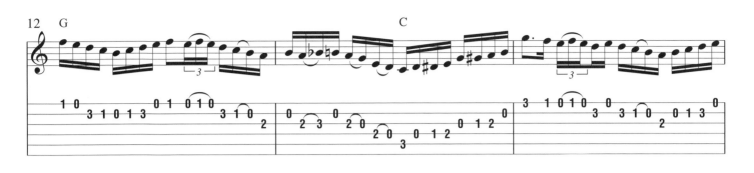

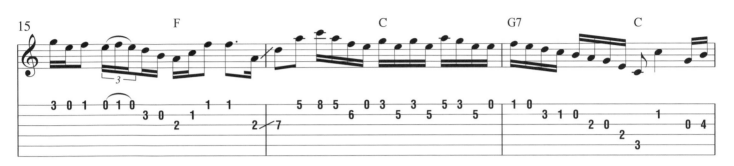

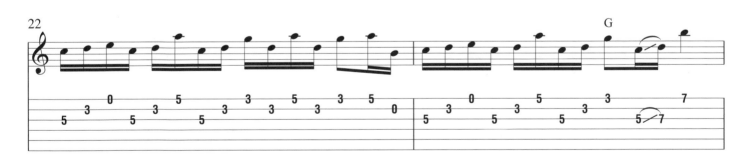

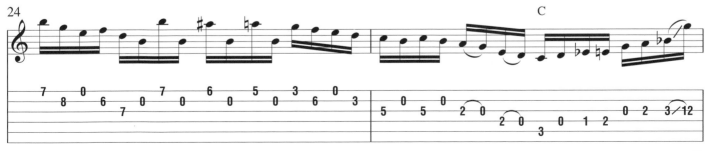

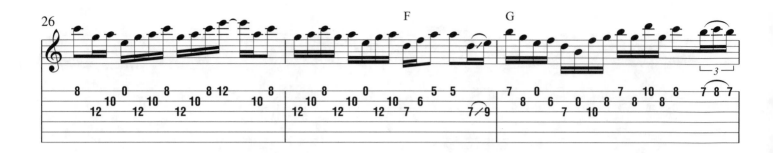

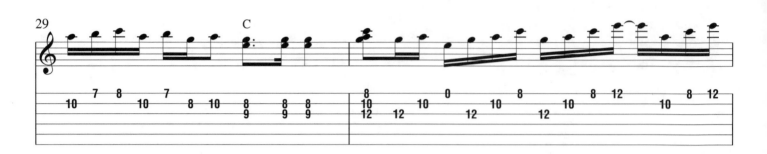

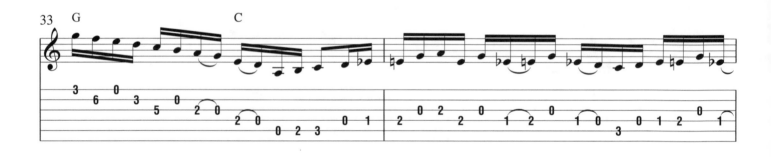

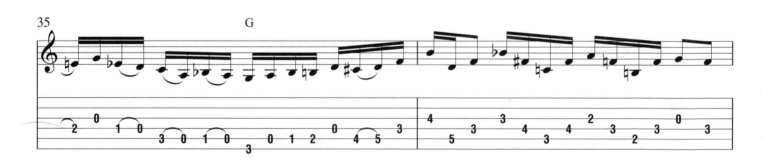

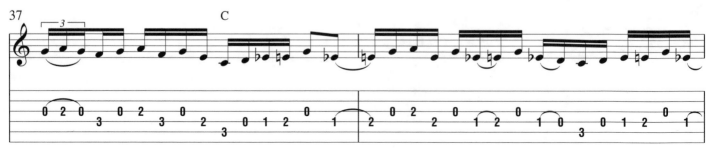

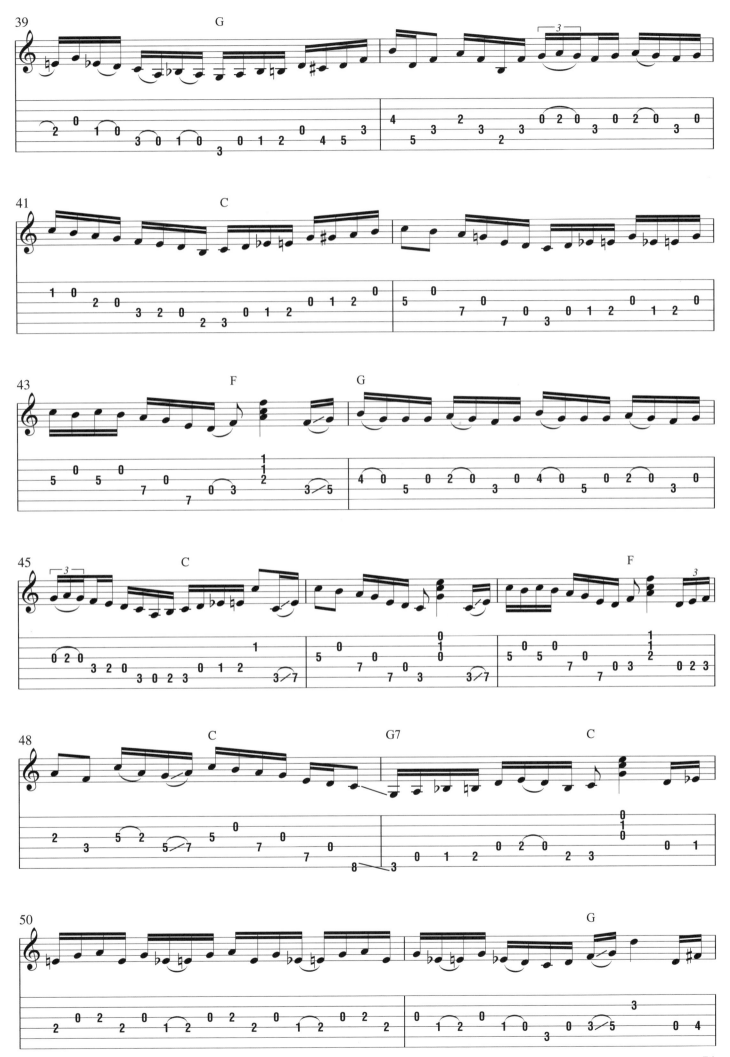

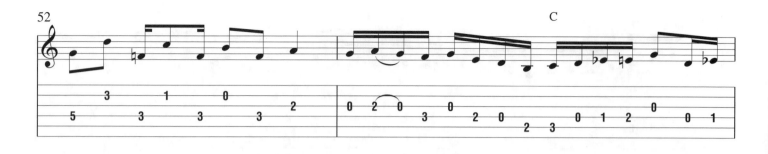

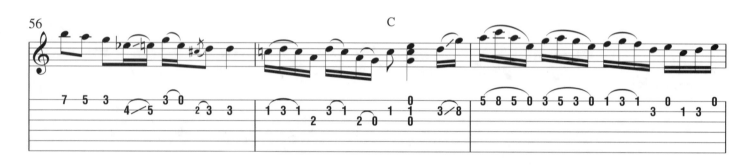

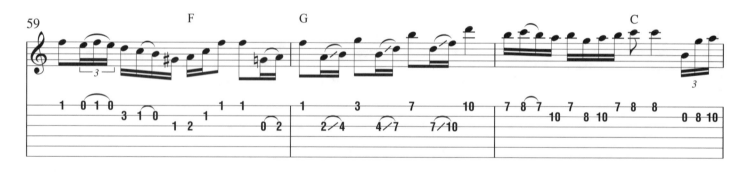

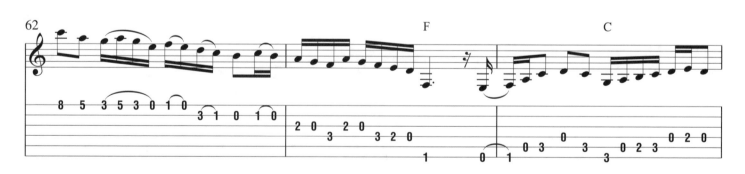

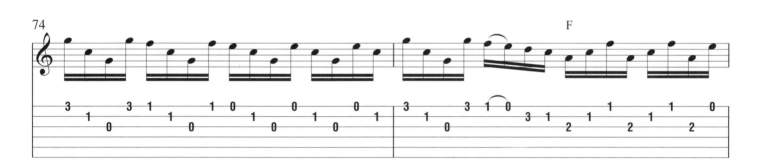

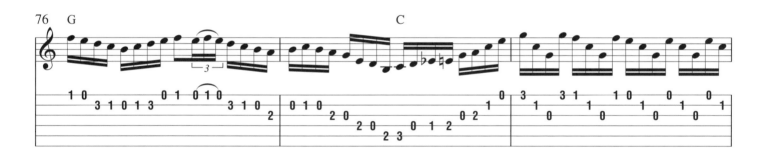

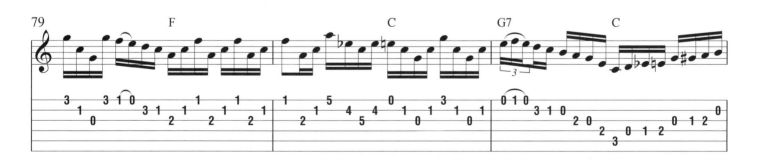

RED HAIRED BOY

Old Time Fiddle Tune

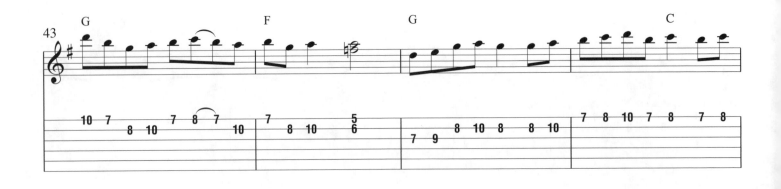

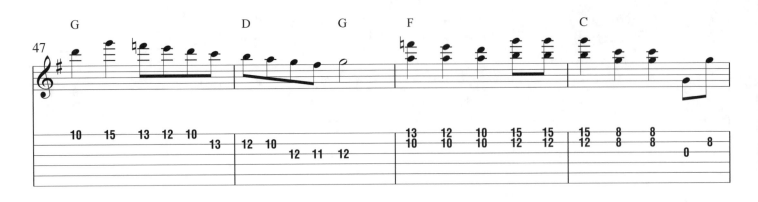

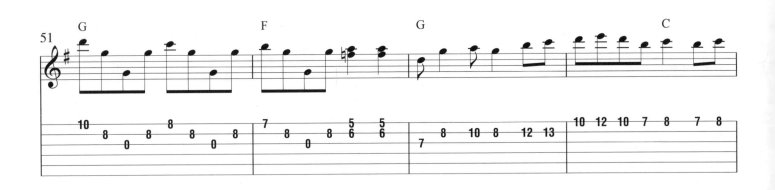

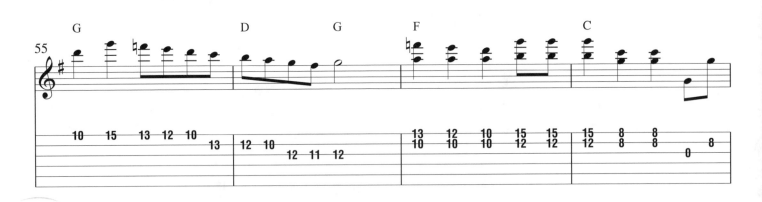

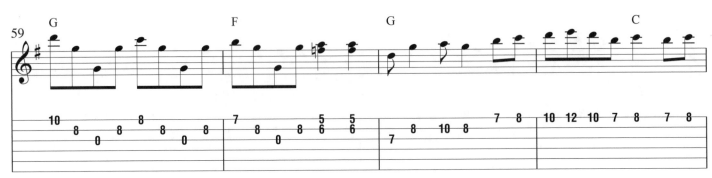

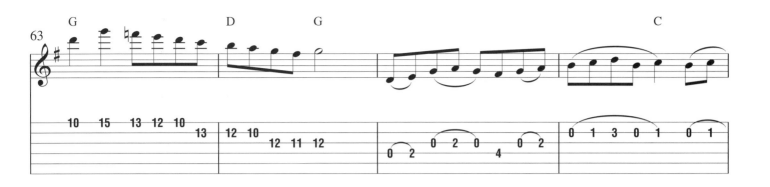

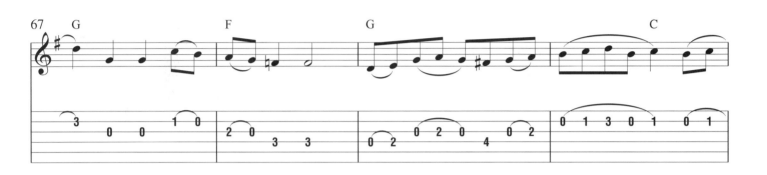

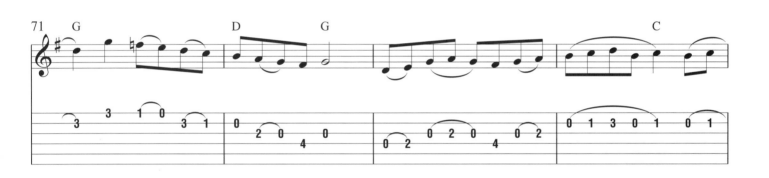

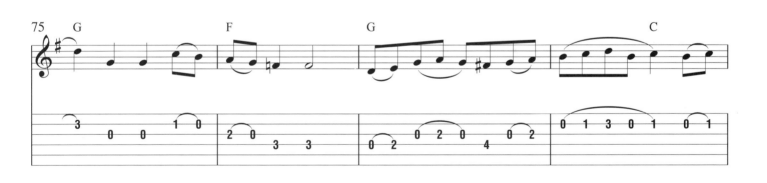

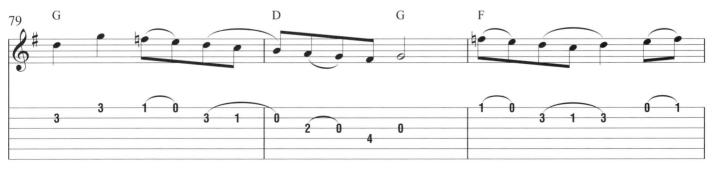

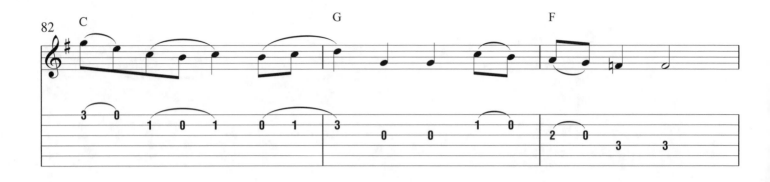

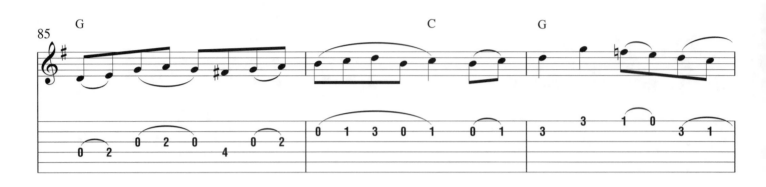

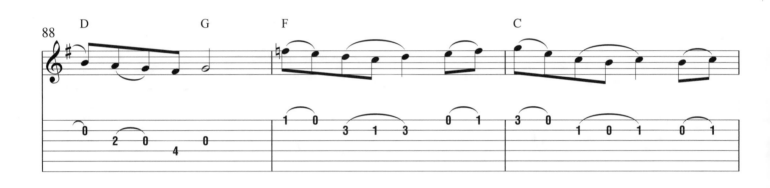

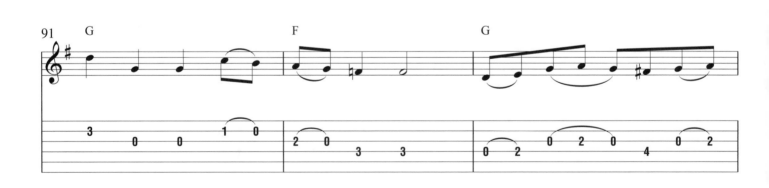

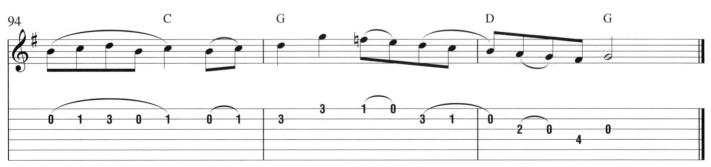

ST. ANNE'S REEL

Traditional Celtic Folksong

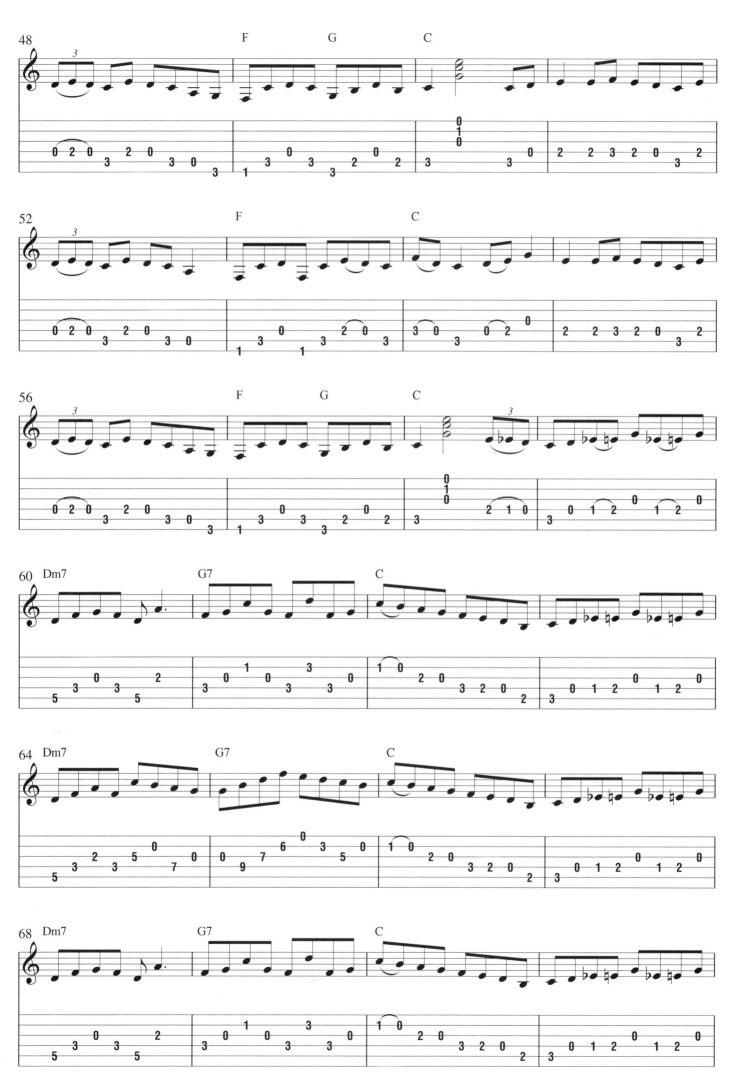

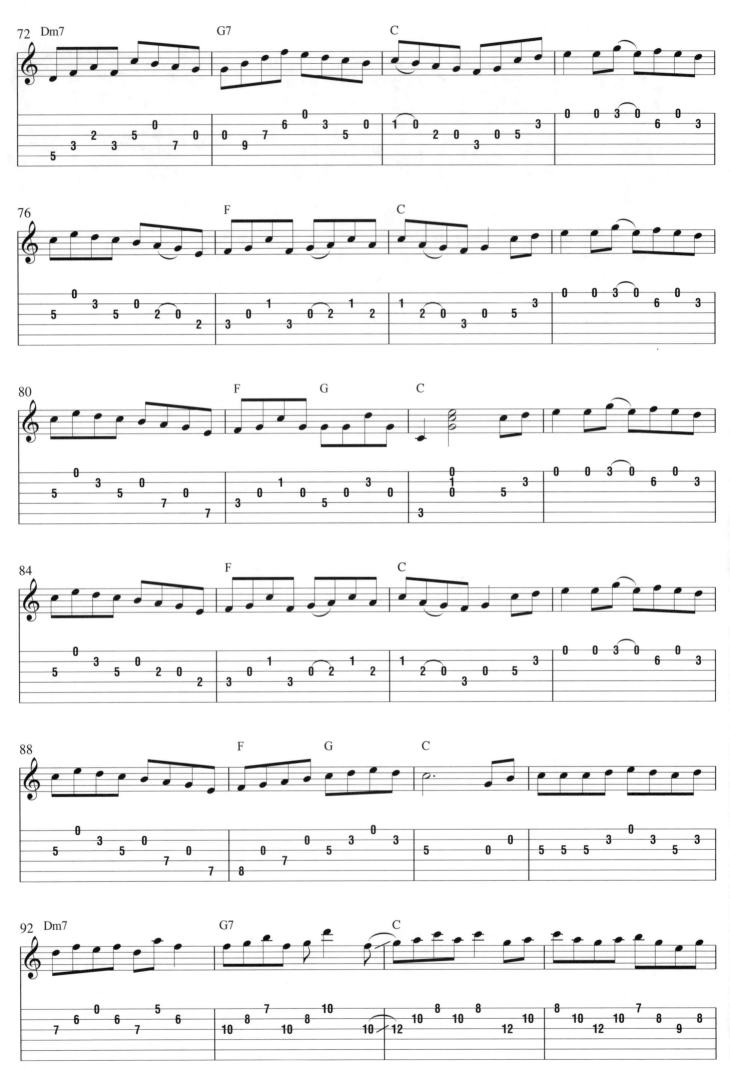

WHISKEY BEFORE BREAKFAST

Old Time

Drop D tuning:
(low to high) D-A-D-G-B-E

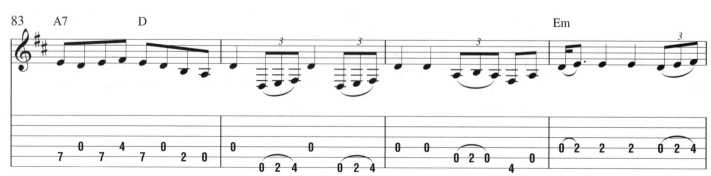

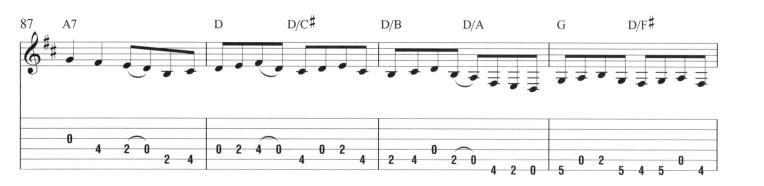

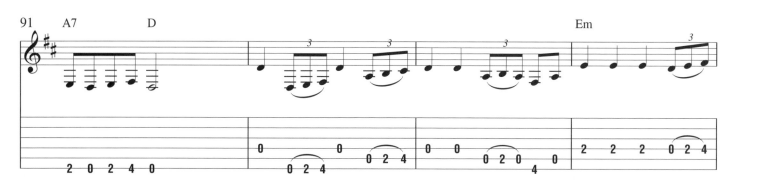

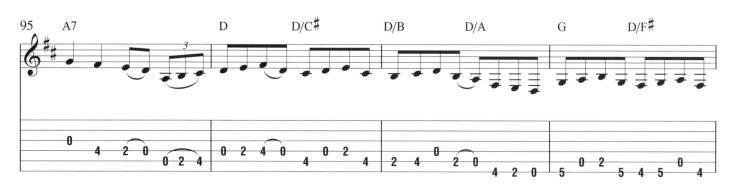

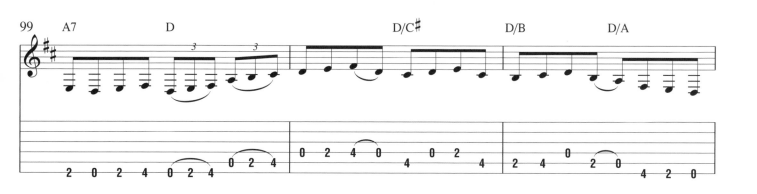

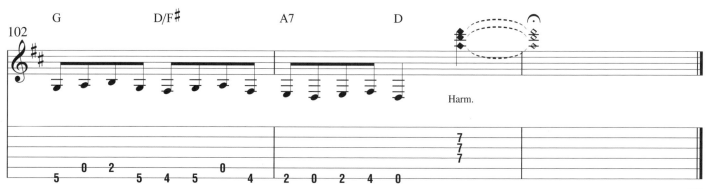

Guitar Notation Legend

Guitar Music can be notated three different ways: on a *musical staff*, in *tablature*, and in *rhythm slashes*.

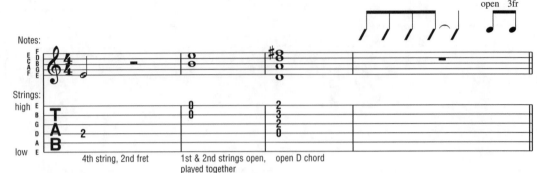

RHYTHM SLASHES are written above the staff. Strum chords in the rhythm indicated. Use the chord diagrams found at the top of the first page of the transcription for the appropriate chord voicings. Round noteheads indicate single notes.

THE MUSICAL STAFF shows pitches and rhythms and is divided by bar lines into measures. Pitches are named after the first seven letters of the alphabet.

TABLATURE graphically represents the guitar fingerboard. Each horizontal line represents a string, and each number represents a fret.

4th string, 2nd fret

1st & 2nd strings open, played together

open D chord

HALF-STEP BEND: Strike the note and bend up 1/2 step.

WHOLE-STEP BEND: Strike the note and bend up one step.

GRACE NOTE BEND: Strike the note and immediately bend up as indicated.

SLIGHT (MICROTONE) BEND: Strike the note and bend up 1/4 step.

BEND AND RELEASE: Strike the note and bend up as indicated, then release back to the original note. Only the first note is struck.

PRE-BEND: Bend the note as indicated, then strike it.

VIBRATO: The string is vibrated by rapidly bending and releasing the note with the fretting hand.

WIDE VIBRATO: The pitch is varied to a greater degree by vibrating with the fretting hand.

HAMMER-ON: Strike the first (lower) note with one finger, then sound the higher note (on the same string) with another finger by fretting it without picking.

PULL-OFF: Place both fingers on the notes to be sounded. Strike the first note and without picking, pull the finger off to sound the second (lower) note.

LEGATO SLIDE: Strike the first note and then slide the same fret-hand finger up or down to the second note. The second note is not struck.

SHIFT SLIDE: Same as legato slide, except the second note is struck.

TRILL: Very rapidly alternate between the notes indicated by continuously hammering on and pulling off.

TAPPING: Hammer ("tap") the fret indicated with the pick-hand index or middle finger and pull off to the note fretted by the fret hand.

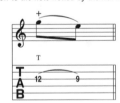

NATURAL HARMONIC: Strike the note while the fret-hand lightly touches the string directly over the fret indicated.

PINCH HARMONIC: The note is fretted normally and a harmonic is produced by adding the edge of the thumb or the tip of the index finger of the pick hand to the normal pick attack.

PICK SCRAPE: The edge of the pick is rubbed down (or up) the string, producing a scratchy sound.

MUFFLED STRINGS: A percussive sound is produced by laying the fret hand across the string(s) without depressing, and striking them with the pick hand.

PALM MUTING: The note is partially muted by the pick hand lightly touching the string(s) just before the bridge.

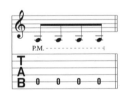

RAKE: Drag the pick across the strings indicated with a single motion.

TREMOLO PICKING: The note is picked as rapidly and continuously as possible.

VIBRATO BAR DIVE AND RETURN: The pitch of the note or chord is dropped a specified number of steps (in rhythm) then returned to the original pitch.

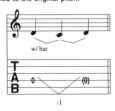

VIBRATO BAR SCOOP: Depress the bar just before striking the note, then quickly release the bar.

VIBRATO BAR DIP: Strike the note and then immediately drop a specified number of steps, then release back to the original pitch.

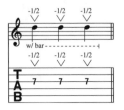

CHERRY LANE MUSIC COMPANY

6 East 32nd Street, New York, NY 10016

Quality in Printed Music

The Magazine You Can Play

Visit the Guitar One web site at **www.guitarone.com**

ACOUSTIC INSTRUMENTALISTS
INCLUDES TAB

Over 15 transcriptions from legendary artists such as Leo Kottke, John Fahey, Jorma Kaukonen, Chet Atkins, Adrian Legg, Jeff Beck, and more.

2500399 Play-It-Like-It-Is Guitar.............................$9.95

THE BEST BASS LINES
INCLUDES TAB

14 super songs: Bohemian Rhapsody • Celebrity Skin • Crash Into Me • Crazy Train • Glycerine • Money • November Rain • Smoke on the Water • Sweet Child O' Mine • What Would You Say • You're My Flavor • and more.

2500311 Play-It-Like-It-Is Bass $14.95

BLUES TAB
INCLUDES TAB

14 songs: Boom Boom • Cold Shot • Hide Away • I Can't Quit You Baby • I'm Your Hoochie Coochie Man • In 2 Deep • It Hurts Me Too • Talk to Your Daughter • The Thrill Is Gone • and more.

2500410 Play-It-Like-It-Is Guitar.........................$14.95

CLASSIC ROCK TAB
INCLUDES TAB

15 rock hits: Cat Scratch Fever • Crazy Train • Day Tripper • Hey Joe • Hot Blooded • Start Me Up • We Will Rock You • You Really Got Me • and more.

2500408 Play-It-Like-It-Is Guitar.........................$14.95

MODERN ROCK TAB
INCLUDES TAB

15 of modern rock's best: Are You Gonna Go My Way • Denial • Hanging by a Moment • I Did It • My Hero • Nobody's Real • Rock the Party (Off the Hook) • Shock the Monkey • Slide • Spit It Out • and more.

2500409 Play-It-Like-It-Is Guitar.........................$14.95

SIGNATURE SONGS
INCLUDES TAB

11 artists' trademark hits: Crazy Train (Ozzy Osbourne) • My Generation (The Who) • Smooth (Santana) • Sunshine Of Your Love (Cream) • Walk This Way (Aerosmith) • Welcome to the Jungle (Guns N' Roses) • What Would You Say (Dave Matthews Band) • and more.

2500303 Play-It-Like-It-Is Guitar.........................$16.95

REFERENCE/INSTRUCTION

BASS SECRETS

WHERE TODAY'S BASS STYLISTS GET TO THE BOTTOM LINE
compiled by John Stix
Bass Secrets brings together 48 columns highlighting specific topics – ranging from the technical to the philosophical – from masters such as Stu Hamm, Randy Coven, Tony Franklin and Billy Sheehan. They cover topics including tapping, walking bass lines, soloing, hand positions, harmonics and more. Clearly illustrated with musical examples.

02500100 ....$12.95

CLASSICS ILLUSTRATED

WHERE BACH MEETS ROCK
by Robert Phillips
Classics Illustrated is designed to demonstrate for readers and players the links between rock and classical music. Each of the 30 columns from *Guitar* highlights one musical concept and provides clear examples in both styles of music. This cool book lets you study moving bass lines over stationary chords in the music of Bach and Guns N' Roses, learn the similarities between "Leyenda" and "Diary of a Madman," and much more!

02500101 ....$9.95

GUITAR SECRETS
INCLUDES TAB

WHERE ROCK'S GUITAR MASTERS SHARE THEIR TRICKS, TIPS & TECHNIQUES
compiled by John Stix
This unique and informative compilation features 42 columns culled from *Guitar* magazine. Readers will discover dozens of techniques and playing tips, and gain practical advice and words of wisdom from guitar masters.

02500099 ....$10.95

IN THE LISTENING ROOM

WHERE ARTISTS CRITIQUE THE MUSIC OF THEIR PEERS
compiled by John Stix
A compilation of 75 columns from *Guitar* magazine, *In the Listening Room* provides a unique opportunity for readers to hear major recording artists remark on the music of their peers. These artists were given no information about what they would hear, and their comments often tell as much about themselves as they do about the music they listened to. Includes candid critiques by music legends like Aerosmith, Jeff Beck, Jack Bruce, Dimebag Darrell, Buddy Guy, Kirk Hammett, Eric Johnson, John McLaughlin, Dave Navarro, Carlos Santana, Joe Satriani, Stevie Ray Vaughan, and many others.

02500097 ....$14.95

Visit Cherry Lane online at **www.cherrylane.com**

LEGENDS OF LEAD GUITAR

THE BEST OF INTERVIEWS: 1995-2000
This is a fascinating compilation of interviews with today's greatest guitarists! From deeply rooted blues giants to the most fearless pioneers, legendary players reveal how they achieve their extraordinary craft.

02500329 ....$14.95

LESSON LAB

This exceptional book/CD pack features more than 20 in-depth lessons. Tackle in detail a variety of pertinent music- and guitar-related subjects, such as scales, chords, theory, guitar technique, songwriting, and much more!

02500330 Book/CD Pack....................................$19.95

NOISE & FEEDBACK

THE BEST OF 1995-2000: YOUR QUESTIONS ANSWERED
If you ever wanted to know about a specific guitar lick, trick, technique or effect, this book/CD pack is for you! It features over 70 lessons on composing • computer assistance • education and career advice • equipment • technique • terminology and notation • tunings • and more.

02500328 Book/CD Pack....................................$17.95

OPEN EARS

A JOURNEY THROUGH LIFE WITH GUITAR IN HAND
by Steve Morse
In this collection of 50 *Guitar* magazine columns from the mid-'90s on, guitarist Steve Morse sets the story straight about what being a working musician *really* means. He deals out practical advice on: playing with the band, songwriting, recording and equipment, and more, through anecdotes of his hard-knock lessons learned.

02500333 ....$10.95

SPOTLIGHT ON STYLE

THE BEST OF 1995-2000: AN EXPLORER'S GUIDE TO GUITAR
This book and CD cover 18 of the world's most popular guitar styles, including: blues guitar • classical guitar • country guitar • funk guitar • jazz guitar • Latin guitar • metal • rockabilly and more!

02500320 Book/CD Pack....................................$19.95

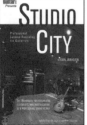

STUDIO CITY

PROFESSIONAL SESSION RECORDING FOR GUITARISTS
by Carl Verheyen
In this collection of colomns from Guitar Magazine, guitarists will learn how to: exercise studio etiquette and act professionally • acquire, assemble and set up gear for sessions • use the tricks of the trade to become a studio hero • get repeat call-backs • and more.

02500195 ....$9.95

1101

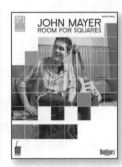